THE ART OF CREATING WEALTH IN REAL ESTATE

Mitanni Spruill-LeSueur

Copyright © 2024 Mitanni Spruill-LeSueur

All rights reserved

No part of this book may be reproduced, or stored in a retrieval system, or transmitted in any form or by any means, electronic, mechanical, photocopying, recording, or otherwise, without express written permission of the publisher.

ISBN: 979-8-218-45811-9

Publisher: Mitanni Spruill-LeSueur

www.TheSpruillAgency.Shop

Printed in the United States of America

To my mother-Beverle Spruill

We are what we repeatedly do. Excellence, then, is not an act, but a habit.

WILL DURANT

CONTENTS

Title Page
Copyright
Dedication
Epigraph
Introduction
The Art of Real Estate   1
How It Started   3
The Fatherless Child   6
The 7-Figure Mindset   8
The 12-year-old Entrepreneur   11
The Socialite   14
The Great 2009 Recession   16
The Big Comeback   19
A Mother's Legacy Restored   22
Acknowledgement   25
About The Author   27

INTRODUCTION

This self-help book is a must-read for anyone looking to increase their sales and productivity. The author shares her harrowing life story of growing up in one of the most dangerous cities in America, and how she overcame obstacles to create wealth in the real estate market.

The book is not just about the author's journey, but also about how she used her experiences to help others achieve their own success. The author's story is inspiring and motivating, and her insights into the real estate market are valuable for anyone looking to make a career change or start a business.

Whether you're a seasoned entrepreneur or just starting out, this book will help you learn from the author's mistakes and successes. You'll gain valuable insights into how to increase your sales and productivity, and how to make the most of your time and resources.

Overall, this book is an excellent investment for anyone looking to improve their business or personal life. With its inspiring story and practical advice, it's sure to help you achieve your goals and become the best version of yourself.

THE ART OF REAL ESTATE

As the tangerine-colored sun rays pierce their way through the almond-colored window shades, I awaken to the soft melodies streaming from my Google alarm clock. My day in the life of real estate begins with a flurry of activity—meetings with high-profile clients in sleek boardrooms, negotiations that could make or break fortunes, and properties changing hands like chess pieces on a board. And then there's me, the poor kid turned self-made heiress to a massive real estate fortune. Who would have known that a child with my background could grow into the hottest Real Estate Broker in the city. I knew I was special and I was determined to prove to myself that anything is possible.

It started as a typical Sunday night, while the city partied in dimly lit nightclubs before returning to work the following day, I managed this time to review my packed upcoming schedule, organize the millions of dollars in sale contracts, and make sure that my real estate brokerage's Realtors are positioned to make a ton of cash this week. At 9 pm I received a phone call from a widely known wealthy professional. I signed a customary NDA, so for privacy reasons, let's call him Adam Beckham. Mr. Beckham lives on the East Coast, and he wants to pay a little over 1,000,000 dollars in cash for a property here in Tennessee. For one million in cash, you can purchase a lot in my town. We have beautiful lakes, fishing ponds, and unique buildings. It's an investor's haven to purchase undervalued properties coupled with a strong rental community. You can make a ton of cash here, so It's no surprise that investors on the East and West Coast pounce on Tennessee's inexpensive real estate opportunities. However, in this case, Mr. Beckham wants to purchase a vacation home here to get away from the hustle and bustle of the East Coast. He is married, so I made sure that the property accommodated his wife's every need as well. I found the property and I sent the Beckham family the details. It was a slam dunk, so we inked the deal and awaited a response from the seller.

It is now 11 pm and as I comb through several emails that were filtered through my spam inbox, I quickly stumble across an email containing an inflated cash offer on my beautiful 3,000 sq ft investment home that my construction company recently completed renovating. My eyes swell in amazement as I review the offer, but then I panic! The email was sent by the investor over two weeks ago and there is a strong possibility that the deal is no longer on the table due to no response from me. I quickly reply to the email and text the investor's Realtor. To my surprise, the investor's agent is working late as well, so we agreed to extend the offer and close in 3 weeks.

HOW IT STARTED

Life was not always this great. The Universe, God, My Higher Self, or whatever name you give it had decided long before I was born that my life to stardom would not be easy. My mom traveled from Los Angeles to Memphis, TN with me and my sister Apuya to visit our family for two weeks during the summer. Memphis was a stark difference from what we were accustomed to in L.A., but we soon adjusted. Our two-week vacation was extended when my mom was asked to help my grandmother take care of my dying grandfather. A nursing home was not an option due to limited funds to pay for one of the nicer senior living communities. I could only imagine the difficult decision that it must have been for my mom to carry the burden of raising two small children alone while being the main caregiver for her father. My mom shared a tiny bed with me and my sister and this became our new home. There were many nights that I was afraid to sleep because my grandmother's home was aggressively infested with brown mice and large roaches. If I had some form of escape at school I could have coped better with my living situation, but the devil worked there disguised as my school teacher. I was a very shy and extremely quiet 8-year-old, but this did not stop my school teacher from physically and mentally abusing me and my classmates in plain sight every day that school year. When she called my name to step over to her desk for those daily sessions of torment, my heart would race with panic and my legs would tremble in fear before going numb. She was pure evil. I learned to suffer in silence in those days because I did not understand the difference between normal and abnormal behavior from adults. I never told my mom about that school year for fear of her being upset with me for what the teacher had done. This is why it is important to have difficult conversations with your children about proper and improper contact with adults. My mom did the best that she could with the cards that she was dealt in life, and I understand that working multiple jobs as a single parent is not easy. My mom is my hero, and she laid the foundation that I built upon today.

When I was about 4 years old, I witnessed death for the first time. It was a very peculiar day when my grandfather slowly withered away at home from kidney failure. I carefully watched as his final breath slipped away like a vapor of smoke, leaving behind a very strange feeling in the house that day. Unexpectedly, my dad was laid off from his job at Universal Studios due to a job strike that had taken place, so he was financially unable to send us to return home. My dad lost our Los Angeles home to foreclosure, and he was forced to sleep in his Mercedes. As a result of this awful news, we continued to live out of a single suitcase back in Memphis in a tiny 2-bedroom home with my grandmother, aunts, uncles, and cousins. I believe that I had fallen into a depression not knowing what depression was as a small child. I refused to talk to anyone except for my mom and sister. Underneath this veil of darkness, I remember falling to my knees on the cracked hardwood floor frantically whispering secret prayers to God to swoop down and save me from this life of sin. I begged for mercy as tears fell down my soft rose-colored cheeks.

Life was hard, but I soon adapted. On any given day, I witnessed prostitutes, pimps, and drug dealers lurking at every corner. There was one day when I was 9 years old, and I had walked to the neighborhood store to grab a few snacks for me and my sister. Unfortunately, I was almost kidnapped. A large man attempted to force me into his brown Cadillac. The store owner saw what was happening, so he grabbed his baseball bat and leaped over customers toward the man as if he was jumping hurdles in the Winter Olympics. He wildly swung the bat while yelling profanities as he chased away the criminal. He saved my life. I ran home as fast as I could to tell my mom and grandmother the frightening news. I know that God spared my life for a great destiny. The good thing about being raised in the shadows of one of the poorest cities in America is that the immense pain and suffering ignites an unbelievable amount of motivation in a few of the chosen ones. I Am the chosen one.

THE FATHERLESS CHILD

My mom had saved enough money to buy airline tickets for me and my sister to visit my dad in Los Angeles when I was 9 years old. During that summer vacation, we had a lot of fun at the beach and Universal Studios theme park. At the beach, my dad noticed that I continued to look down at the ground as I walked. My dad told me to always look up with confidence and to never look down. That lesson reminded me to always be confident in who I am no matter the situations looming over my life. Today, I continue to use this advice in my professional career. My mom finally told me a few years ago that the reason why we did not move back with my dad as a family in Los Angeles during that summer vacation was that when they locked eyes at the airport, she realized that she no longer loved him enough to salvage the marriage. Unfortunately, a bond was never formed between my dad and me after that great summer vacation. The next time I laid eyes on my dad was at his funeral during my last year in high school.

When life throws you lemons, make a delicious ass lemonade. When I was 12 years old my mom was approved to purchase her first home not far from my grandmother's house. It was a huge celebration because we finally had more living space. As you stepped in our front door, the sounds of gunshots were immediately drowned out by the magical ambiance that my mom created. On any given day you could smell homemade cakes and pies baking in the oven. Life was turning around for the good. Our home was beautifully decorated in black and gold colors with exotic Egyptian artifacts displayed throughout. My mother loved Egyptian history and she passed Egyptian birth names to me and my sister. Many years later through DNA testing, we discovered that we are related to one of the Pharaohs of Egypt. My daydreams on the playground of being royalty seemed to have come to life for a short moment in time on that day.

THE 7-FIGURE MINDSET

"Congratulations on your closing!" I excitedly screamed while popping a bottle of Dom Pérignon champagne at the closing table with my investor! We closed our first apartment and office building deal together and business was expected to keep climbing non-stop.

I adopted a very basic investment strategy of investing in real estate in those early years of selling real estate that is proven to work just as well today as they did for me back then. I highly suggest meeting with a licensed financial advisor for investment advice. The strategies listed in this section are what helped me when I entered into the investment space. I know it will help you as well. I will share them here:

> 1) If you have little to no cash, you must think in smaller increments to simply get started. When you are building capital to invest in your first property take 20% of your monthly income and save it for one year. Do not touch your savings for any reason. After one year, go to your local tax office and request a list of their tax sale properties. Oftentimes, there will be properties with back taxes owed for only a few thousand dollars. Buy whatever you can afford or find a partner to split the deal with you to make the deal

affordable. Next, clean the place up, trim the trees, mow the grass, and remove all trash. If you do not have enough capital to renovate it for retail sale or rental income you will want to sell it to a bigger investor for no less than about a 45% profit. **Example**: $14,000.00 purchase price to include taxes, $500 for cleanup, and other miscellaneous costs for a total of $14,500.00 acquisition cost. The list price to investors should be about $21,025. This should give you a profit of $6,525.00. Rinse and repeat.

2) If you do not have income to save for investing, then your situation becomes more complicated. However, it is doable. You will still need to go to the tax assessor's office for the list of tax properties, but instead of paying cash for these properties, you will need to contact the homeowner of record who is behind on property tax payments and ask the homeowner to make a deal. Offer to help secure financing to pay off their back taxes, offer them a moving van and an extra thousand or so dollars to vacate the property at the closing. Explain in detail that you have investors that you partner with who may be interested in teaming up with you to deliver on the agreements made. Do not make any promises but offer a path to relieving them of this burden of debt, avoid a foreclosure on their credit, and receive some extra cash in their pockets when the deal closes. Discuss how your offer is the better option vs the local county office foreclosing on their home for back taxes. Be honest and transparent. Many of the local county offices in America are notorious for doing this to poor families, but with your ambition, you can turn a bad situation into a good one. Once you are under contract you will need to deliver results fast. You should team up with your local Realtor association and request to add a property into their MLS system without a representation agreement if allowed in your state. There should only be a small fee for this service versus paying a full commission to a realtor. However, it is ideal to use a

realtor if you can afford one because this will save you time and effort with a trained professional on your side. Once your property is listed in your local MLS you will receive calls from investors wanting to view the property. It will be a good idea to have a lockbox on the home with a key unless you prefer to be present for all showings. Once you receive an offer for your interest in the property, always include a non-refundable deposit of 1% of the sales price. This will add an extra layer of protection for you and deter buyers who are not serious. At closing, fulfill your obligations to the homeowner and pay off all debt as promised. Rinse and repeat.

3) If you're a realtor aiming to break into the six or seven-figure club; this book is your guide. Start by setting a target for how many real estate conversations you need to have before converting to a sale. Typically, only 1% of cold calls to Expired Listings will convert. Door-knocking is another essential tactic, but arm yourself with valuable data, door hangers, and goodies before hitting the pavement. Map out your target neighborhood, compile CMA reports for each home, and deliver them personally. If there are no expired listings, get creative—use open houses as conversation starters when the homeowner opens the door to speak with you. Forget about costly online leads; focus on proven methods like monthly mailers, calling expired listings, or networking at popular coffee shops. Whatever strategy you choose, stick with it consistently for at least six months. By then, you'll be able to assess your progress and make necessary adjustments. Aim to have at minimum 2-4 closings per month within the dollar figure range that you wish to net each year. If you desire a 7-figure annual income, you should close 2-4 seven-figure homes each month on average.

THE 12-YEAR-OLD ENTREPRENEUR

My childhood made me who I am today, because navigating life as a 12-year-old in a rough neighborhood required a lot of mental strength and impeccable negotiating skills, both of which came naturally to me. I was in the 7th grade, and it was the end of the school year. There were no planned activities for me and my sister because my mom had to work 2 to 3 jobs on any given week. I had a great idea to make money which involved selling bologna and cheese sandwiches, sodas, and chips from our home to the neighborhood kids. I was not old enough to get a real job, so I decided to work for myself. My plan was kept a secret because it was conditioned upon my mom not uncovering my covert sales operation. The food that I sold was purchased by my mom to keep me and my sister fed while she was out working long hours each day. Nonetheless, business that summer was great. I had a wonderful marketing plan as well. My marketing plan involved advertising the food items as combo meals to increase profitability. This encouraged customers to buy three food items at a special discounted rate instead of buying only one item. I made a pocket full of cash that summer and I had big dreams of expanding my love for business further.

Unfortunately, being raised by a single mother on the wrong side of town had its consequences: I found myself hanging with the wrong crowd at the wrong places and getting into a whirlwind of trouble. My closest friends were no longer the church kids with whom I sang in the church choir on Sundays. I was only 14 years old, but I felt like I was 30. I soon became a teenage mom, and I was scared half to death because I was having a child before graduation. I gave birth to my first child, and I named him Cinque. He was my entire world, so I distanced myself from friends who did not benefit my higher purpose. I could not allow my baby to experience the trauma that I experienced as a child. My new mission in life was in full throttle and I began to train myself on how to become a successful businesswoman one day. My path transcended personal achievements; it was a relentless mission to uplift my community and restore my mother's legacy. My mother sacrificed her entire young life to raise me and my sister as a single mother and I was determined to repay her for her sacrifices.

On my 18th birthday, I decided to enroll myself into the local community college where I later graduated with a Pre-Law associate's degree. I transferred my college credits to the University of Memphis where I studied International Politics, Law, and other business courses. While completing coursework at the university I decided to propel myself by looking for a more respected career in business. I was inspired by my co-worker's success as a builder's agent at Bowden Home Builders, so I seized the opportunity to take the real estate test the following week.

I had prepared myself for the biggest interview in my life. I arrived early at the home builder's office, and I was ready to ace the test and become a real estate agent. I was dressed in my best powder blue two-piece pantsuit, and I carried my black leather briefcase to show that I meant business. I passed the real estate test, but unfortunately, the homebuilder asked me to come back when I was a few years older. This was the first of many age discrimination hurdles that I had encountered as I ventured into the world of real estate. The good news is that I do not easily take no for an answer. Each rejection ignites a burning flame within me, elevating me higher towards my goals. I wanted to buy my first investment property shortly after becoming a licensed Realtor, but I had a major problem; I was broke. My financial situation did not stop me from planning my next move. My next goal soon became to sell a few homes and save my commission checks to start my investing venture. My first check was for $4,551, which I used towards the purchase of my first investment property. I bought and sold that first house to another investor in less than 2 weeks for a 50% profit. Next, I managed the renovation of the home for this same investor for a sizable fee and he also allowed me to list the house for sale. This one property allowed me to get paid four different ways in less than two months.

THE SOCIALITE

As a realtor in my early twenties made me the talk of the town, sparking both admiration and envy. I'll never forget my first taste of high society at an upscale nightclub—it wasn't your typical college party scene. It was the kind of place where you'd see rich NBA stars arriving in a convoy of sleek black Suburbans, commanding attention like military VIPs. Stepping inside, I witnessed money raining down as if it were confetti, a surreal spectacle of excess and extravagance. I loved my new lifestyle, and I enjoyed the fruits of my labor. At these night outings, I rubbed shoulders with some influential tycoons and esteemed politicians, many of whom I would later do business with. I met Aubrey, the owner of a popular downtown store where many of the Memphis Grizzlies players shopped. Aubrey was a very intelligent man and he introduced me to my first client Mr. Vasquez on the Memphis Grizzlies NBA team. I would pick up Mr. Vasquez from the Westin Hotel during the off-season and we toured homes for a few hours. Mr. Vasquez was so impressed with my service that he told his teammates about me. Before I knew it, I was showing half of the NBA team properties. It was a very rewarding experience. One gentleman by the name of Stanley worked for a very large Fortune 1000 insurance firm. As a token of appreciation, he would give me courtside seats to some of the best NBA Grizzlies games. I later became the go-to realtor to many of the NBA players on the team. It all felt surreal like I was living in a dream. Every weekend was a whirlwind of parties as if we were trying to cram a lifetime of pleasure into each fleeting moment. There were endless charity events and fancy dinners. It all seemed like a dream. While I danced the night away, an economic storm was brewing in the background and this lavish lifestyle would soon cost me a huge fortune. However, my much older and wiser counterparts were smart as they prepared to brace themselves for the worst recession in the history of America.

THE GREAT 2009 RECESSION

It was the summer of 2009, and The Great Recession was in full throttle. Over 6 million families lost their homes to foreclosure and billion-dollar companies like Lehman Brothers and Crysler were forced into bankruptcy. Home sales plummeted and the real estate market had lost its pulse of survival. Reflecting on those days, I recalled witnessing prominent Realtors vanish from the industry to trade their high-level Realtor status for the 9-5 grind. It was a complete disaster. The Obama Administration tried its best to fit the pieces together into this over-complicated jigsaw puzzle. I remember sitting at my dining room table and hearing the echo of my then-boyfriend urging me to get out of the real estate business because he lost faith in the industry. For a split second, I came to a fork in the road to decide what to do next with my career. My bills were beginning to pile up, I did not know when my next commission check was coming, and I lost over half of the equity in my home due to the poor economy. While sitting at my dining room table a light bulb had gone off in my mind and I was reminded that I never went down without a fight. In that same moment, I made the drastic decision to grab my boxing gloves and open my real estate brokerage The Spruill Agency, formerly named Spruill Luxury Realty LLC. It may have sounded like suicide to bystanders, but it was my only solution to not giving up. Sometimes bold risky decisions are what separates the rich from the poor. That decision at my dining room table catapulted me to an unimaginable height. It was one of the best business decisions that I have ever made in my life.

In the fall of 2009, I proudly opened the doors to my real estate brokerage. Bursting with excitement, I immersed myself deeper into my new workspace. Nights blurred into mornings as I poured my heart and soul into building my empire. Every spare moment became an opportunity to visit my new business sanctuary, whether it was a quick detour on the way to a dinner party, between property showings, or simply passing by on my way to a friend's house. It was one of the proudest moments of my career while one of the most terrible economic downturns of the century loomed over my head at every turn.

There was a time when I was teaching my sister Apuya about real estate investing. I wanted her to get into the business with me so that we could take the city by storm. I found a property that was occupied by our mother's hairstylist, and he was ready to sell it. I thought this would be a great opportunity for my sister to get into the real estate investing business as an investor. She had great credit, and I structured the deal to help her with the down payment. I knew that this would be a great opportunity for her. We closed and my sister was the proud owner of her first investment property that she would rent and receive passive income from each month. However, this situation only worked out for a short period because the tenant decided to break the lease and move out early. My sister decided to eventually list the condo for sale. Once listed a wonderful investor became interested and submitted an offer. This was one of the biggest turning points in my career besides opening my firm because this investor would turn out to be one of the biggest investors in my career. She was highly intelligent, owned hundreds of properties and she had a lot of cash to spend. Not only did she purchase my sister's condo, but she went on to purchase many other properties from me. She allowed me to sell other off-market commercial properties for her and she later began purchasing multiple luxury homes in cash.

The commission to my new firm exponentially increased. The homes that she purchased had neighbors who were top executives at FedEx, NBA players for the Memphis Grizzlies, well-known singers, famous actors, and the list went on. This opportunity allowed me to meet many influential people and my name in the real estate world became synonymous with high-level real estate sales and service. I had magically turned The Great Recession from being my enemy to a close friend. The lesson that I learned from that experience was to always change your perspective of a not-so-good environment to match the dream that you have in your heart. It will take some effort and time on your part, but if you do the work, you have positive thinking, you can turn any situation around for your good. The Universe will move people, places, and things to manifest your deepest desires.

THE BIG COMEBACK

It was just an ordinary weekend morning at home, and I decided to take a moment to meditate. After I finished meditating, an impulse nudged me toward my home office closet. I wandered in, not quite sure what I was searching for until my eyes landed on it: my old vision board, tucked away for years. I hurried to the scrolled poster board eager to revisit the dreams I had once mapped out. To my amazement, almost every dream that I had pasted to my vision board had come true. It was like magic—manifestation in action. I recall the days when my very small zero-lot home (a home without a true front yard) was just a cozy spot for me and my son. I reflected on the many years I spent studying the Law of Attraction philosophers such as Echart Tolle, Dale Carnegie, Rhonda Byrne, and many others. I remember when I often found myself drawn to the gated communities of the affluent, dreaming of the day that I would call one of those grand mansions my own. As a Realtor, we have access to many neighborhoods, so I used to drive to one of the most expensive gated communities in town and I park my car near the courtyard. I would find a cozy seat on the park bench and immerse myself in visions of owning one of the massive homes nearby. I would do this for about 30 minutes a few times a week. Little did I know then, that those dreams were planting seeds of destiny. Fast forward to the present, and here I am, tears welling in my eyes as I realize I'm living in a home similar to the one on my vision board. Today, my home boasts over 6,000 square feet with three mini fishing lakes sitting on over 20 acres of land—more than I could have ever imagined. I have come a very long way from living out of a suitcase with my mom and sister many years ago as a child. My vision board is a reminder of the power of visualization, of believing in the dreams that would one day manifest. So, to anyone out there yearning to expand their horizons, I say: start with a vision board. Whether it's a digital app on your phone or the good old-fashioned poster board adorned with clippings from magazines and printed photos, it's a magical portal to your destiny!

I went on to have many other accomplishments throughout my career. I opened a commercial finance company, and a construction company and I started a non-profit www.Give2CLWCA.org that helps underprivileged families with basic living necessities. My goal for the non-profit is to raise enough donations to build apartments and tiny homes for underprivileged families at no cost to the family. My sister Apuya serves as the Secretary on the non-profit board and she is currently working towards joining my real estate team as a Transactional Coordinator-Realtor at my brokerage. My real estate brokerage is expanding to other parts of the country as well and we are always looking for new talent with fresh and creative ideas. One of my biggest accomplishments is watching my firstborn son grow up and create his path in life. Also, I married my long-time boyfriend Jeremy LeSueur and we have two beautiful daughters that we named Legacy and Majesty.

As I previously mentioned, philanthropy resonates deeply with me, so my real estate brokerage holds a charity event each year to help raise funds for St. Jude Children's Research Hospital. Our most recent event was a tea party-themed social gathering for the local community. We had several speakers within the real estate industry share golden nuggets on how to successfully purchase and sell real estate in today's market. It was a beautifully decorated event with an assortment of tea party-styled treats. The attire was tea party-inspired black tie and the event sold out online within a few days. The Memphis Business Journal, a highly respected business publication, published an article about my event on their website. I encourage all business professionals to curate positive local events to bring awareness to important topics within your community and specific industries. By doing so, you will be known as the go-to expert within your profession.

A MOTHER'S LEGACY RESTORED

My mother's legacy has finally been restored. She focuses her time on writing screenplays, and she no longer struggles financially. Thinking back on my childhood from the perspective of my current situation, I now understand why I went through all the trauma and heartbreak that I endured growing up being raised by a single mom and not having the adequate resources that many other children had allowed me to depend on my intellect, my resources, and my strength. I knew as a child that if I wanted something that my mother could not provide, I had to go and get it myself. This level of independence as a child sparked the entrepreneur side of my DNA into activation mode. We all have that activation button patiently waiting to be pushed, but sometimes it takes the bad moments in life to force you to see that if you dig down deep enough that button can and will be activated in your life. There is not an obstacle or a mountain too high that can stop you from your God-given destiny. Believe in yourself and remember the power given to you by the most high God and know that there is not a situation too hard to overcome. We all have natural given talents and all we must do is remember who we are. This is your cue to think about your childhood and remember what you enjoyed the most doing. Once you remember you will have the key to unlock your future destiny. The goal of this book is not only for me to get my life's work on paper to share with the world, but to grant you the ability to remember who you truly are.

I love you and I am excited about your new journey to creating wealth in real estate.

ACKNOWLEDGEMENT

I owe my fullest gratitude to my mother Beverle Spruill who passed the gift of writing to me as I was formed in her womb. This book has been a creation waiting to be manifested for many years. I told my mother when I was in highschool that I wanted to write a book about my life but I did not know where to start or how it would end. Her response was that I had not yet lived long enough to tell my story but when the time was right my thoughts would flow.

This book is only a small snippet of my highs and lows, my triumphs and defeats but it is compact enough to enjoy in one sitting yet long enough to give you a genuine glimpse into my life as an entrepreneur in real estate.

I want to thank my husband Jeremy LeSueur for being understanding for the many nights and weekends that I spent drafting the details of this book. I want to thank my children Cinque, Legacy, and Majesty for coming into my life at key moments that helped shape and define who I am today as a woman, mother, wife, daughter, sister, and friend.

I am very honored to have an amazing real estate team at my brokerage The Spruill Agency. The realtors that work for me have been truly amazing at providing the best service to our clients.

And thank you to my clients and friends who supported me along the way. Your loyalty will never go unnoticed.

ABOUT THE AUTHOR

Mitanni Spruill-Lesueur

Meet Mitanni Spruill-LeSueur, a trailblazer whose journey to greatness is nothing short of inspiring. Armed with a passion for real estate and an unwavering determination, Mitanni set out to redefine the industry norms.

Starting from humble beginnings, Mitanni faced initial challenges but used them as stepping stones rather than stumbling blocks. She immersed herself in learning the intricacies of the market, dedicating long hours to mastering the art of negotiation and understanding the unique needs of her clients.

Mitanni's commitment to excellence quickly caught the attention of both clients and colleagues. Known for her unparalleled work ethic and ability to turn challenges into opportunities, Mitanni became the go-to real estate broker for those seeking a personalized and high-value experience.

Embracing technology and innovation, Mitanni was an early adopter of virtual real estate platforms, recognizing the potential to reach a global clientele. Leveraging these tools, she seamlessly connected buyers with their dream properties and sellers with qualified buyers, all while maintaining a personal touch that set her apart.

Her dedication to her clients went beyond transactions; Mitanni became a trusted advisor, guiding them through every step of the real estate journey. Her genuine care and attention to detail resulted in not just satisfied clients, but raving fans who referred her services to friends and family.

As Mitanni's reputation soared, so did her success. She earned accolades for her achievements, with her name becoming synonymous with excellence in the real estate world. Mitanni Spruill-LeSueur wasn't just a Realtor; she was a symbol of determination, hard work, and the relentless pursuit of greatness.

She is a graduate of The University of Memphis, a member of the prestigious National Association of Realtors, Tennessee Association of Realtors, Northwest Mississippi Association of Realtors, Memphis Area Association of Realtors, National Association of Home Builders, Memphis Area Minority Contractors Association, West Tennessee Association of Home Builders, Home Builders Association of Tennessee, and The Greater Memphis Chamber of Commerce. Mitanni heads a non-profit foundation www.Give2CLWCA.org, and she volunteers her time to various church, school, and non-profit organizations, including St. Jude Children's Research Hospital.

Today, Mitanni's story serves as an inspiration for aspiring real estate professionals, a testament to the fact that passion, coupled with hard work and innovation, can propel anyone to achieve greatness in the dynamic world of real estate.

www.ingramcontent.com/pod-product-compliance
Lightning Source LLC
Chambersburg PA
CBHW051949160426
43198CB00013B/2370